WHO IS GINGER?

WHO IS GINGER?

A TRUE TAIL BY

Joy Peeler

Charleston, SC
www.PalmettoPublishing.com

Who is Ginger?

First Edition

Paperback ISBN: 979-8-8229-1082-9

Dedication:

TO FATHER TED AND GINGER,
thank you for the opportunity to share
the life you and Ginger have with others.

Dogs speak, but only to those who listen.

—Orhan Pamuk

Preface

I first met Ginger and Father Ted during the COVID pandemic. I searched online for a church service and found Father Ted's lovely church. I enjoyed his sermons, continuing to watch every Sunday. One Sunday, a cute golden-brown dog entered the screen. I began tuning in each Sunday, anxious to see what Ginger would be up to next. I wouldn't be disappointed. I hope you enjoy Ginger and Father Ted's story.

I am Ginger, a golden-brown dog, and I have a special story to tell you. You know dogs live in many different places and with many different people. I live with a Catholic priest named Father Ted. He is the head of a lovely church. Keep reading, and you will see how we met.

One Friday each month, Father Ted would visit a lady who was sick and could not leave her house to go to church. The lady had a beagle dog named Daisy, and each time Father visited the lady, he noticed how well-behaved and friendly Daisy was. Father told the lady, "Daisy is the nicest dog I've ever met. If you ever want to get rid of her, give her to me." I think he was kidding, but I know my mother was a very nice dog.

Guess what! Daisy had puppies, six of them, and I was the smallest, the "runt" of the litter. The lady called Father and asked if he wanted one of the puppies. Father hurried over to the lady's house to take a look. The day we met, I slowly crept over to him, wagging my tail. I felt a little tap on my head. I didn't bark. Father decided he wanted me, so off we went. The lady had already given me a name, and Father thought of changing it. Rose and Ripper were two of the names he thought of. In the end, he decided my pretty color made Ginger the perfect name.

I was only a puppy, and puppies like to play. Father liked to play with me. Of course, all I wanted to do was play. Whenever we would play, I heard sounds as he gently patted my head. I am a dog, and I don't understand words. Father's face shows me he is happy, too. I even get soft pats in church while Father is doing work inside.

I love being close to Father.

Afternoon is a fun time to take walks in the park. Father and I say hello to people passing by. I carefully walk over to them, hoping for a little tap on my head. I never jump up on them. I see many pretty flowers and bushes all around the park. I keep my head down. I'm always looking for something hiding under the rocks and pebbles. Beautiful flowers are my favorites, especially the bright-red ones. I sniff at those, and sometimes they smell good.

I love sniffing.

I want to tell you something very important. Father Ted served in the army before we met. He helped soldiers who needed someone to listen. When he returned home from service, he often felt sad for no reason or angry for the smallest reason. He still did a good job at his church. I like to think once I came home with him, things changed. Maybe he just wanted a friend to keep him company.

I certainly did that.

In the beginning of my new life, I liked following Father around, as I felt a bit shy and didn't want to be too far from him.

Sunday is church day, and lots of people are around. Father decided to get me used to seeing so many people. He gently tied a leash to a pole by the front door of the church. At first, I was a bit scared, but soon soft pats on my head and little treats made me feel much better. I never jump on people or growl loudly.

I am a well-behaved dog.

In time, Father allowed me to stay with him after church and say goodbye to everyone. I always see lots of smiles on faces when I am there. If I get tired, I sit down close to Father. Of course, I wait patiently.

I like seeing everyone.

One day, Father took me to meet people work-
ing in the church office. I heard lots of noise
and saw people busy doing work for church.
People always stopped to say hello to me, I
greeted them with a little wag of my tail. If
Father stays busy for a long time, I can take a
nap in the church office until he is finished.
I don't really like staying alone for too long.
I have a doggie bed in the office. My dog bed
is so pretty and very soft. I think Father piled
two or three of my beds together. Oh my, very
soft indeed!

I like taking naps.

Puppies grow and learn very fast. I made a few mistakes growing up. I like to chew holes in Father's socks. At first, he got angry and yelled at me. I felt sad, and I think he felt sad, too.

I was very sad.

I am about to tell you one of my second-favorite things about living with Father. There is an elementary school for boys and girls close to our church. One day, my ears perked up hearing little voices coming from the playground next to the school. I started wagging my tail, and Father knew I wanted to head over that way. We walked over toward the school building and quietly down the long hall. I could hear children whispering, "Here comes Ginger, Father Ted's new dog." Father told me not to bark and disturb the children; they were learning their lessons. I loved seeing the boys and girls and wanted to go every day.

Boys and girls make me happy.

Father and I follow a routine each day. First, we unlock the church and head over to the school building. One day, Father was taking too long to take me over to school, so I decided to dash over to the school by myself. Walking down the hall and peeking in classrooms, I saw boys and girls quietly sitting at their desks listening to the teacher. I heard them whisper, "There's Ginger." Of course, I was very quiet, remembering what Father had told me.

I didn't get in trouble.

I love going inside the church. I can't go in when the people are having the service because you know dogs are not allowed in church, but Father often takes me in while he is preparing for services. There are so many beautiful things to see in church. I love the statues and colorful lights. Right before church begins, I go into the residence; that is what they call where Father and I live. I am allowed to come out after church, and as Father says, I "work the crowd."

**I am a popular
member of the staff.**

Father always thinks of making me comfortable. He places a pretty rug near the altar and glowing lights. The first time I saw the little rug, I thought this must be for me.

I enjoy resting on my little rug.

We have music in our church, and Father likes to play the piano. I think the sounds are kind of loud. You know dogs have very good hearing.

I love the sound of the music.

Father wears brightly colored robes in church, and I actually see the colors. Some people say dogs only see black and white, but I see robes of pink and green. People sing in church, and one of the ladies wears a colorful purple robe and often pats my head gently.

I love bright colors.

One day, when I was five years old, we had to move to a new church, a bigger one in a town far away. We said goodbye to everyone in the church, the workers in the office, and the teachers and children in the school. Everyone was very sad to see us go. Father and I were very sad, too.

I didn't want to leave.

In the beginning, I was upset living at the new church. I found everything so different. People in the church office looked different. The children in the school would get so excited, I felt scared. Really, nothing was the same. When I stayed in the office, I cried and howled. Left alone in the house, I cried and howled even more. All of this made Father sad. Everyone did their best to cheer me up, but I still missed my old friends and the good old days.

I hoped the days would get better.

Father and I continued with our daily routine at the new church, opening the doors of the church and heading over to the school. In time, children learned to be calm and gentle with me, and I felt calmer and more comfortable at our new home. I realized I just had to get used to things that are new. People in our new church were almost like the people in our old church. All the people treated me nicely.

I continue to be happy.

My new town has a nice park, and when we have time, Father says, "Ginger, let's head out for a walk in the park." I let Father know I am ready for a walk. My job is chasing away squirrels, rabbits, deer, geese, and groundhogs. I enjoy every minute of my work.

I love our walks.

So, you see, Father Ted and I have a very busy life. Father has much work to do, and he often needs a little vacation. I can't always join him. People in our church family take care of me. They are called "dog sitters." Many different people offer, and I like going to their homes and seeing different flowers and bushes. One time, I got to sit outside by a little pretty blue pool.

I like seeing different things.

Even though it is kind of an adventure staying with different people in different places, I do miss Father. I don't think it is very long before he returns to pick me up and take me home.

I always hug him.

There is one more thing I want to tell you about my life with Father Ted. Remember I told you what my second-favorite thing is? I guess you are wondering what my favorite thing is. At the end of each day, when it's time to go to bed, Father puts his arm around me and says, "Ginger, you are a good dog, and everybody loves you because you are so nice."

After hearing that, I curl up and go to sleep. When I awake, I am happy, Father is happy, and people in our church family are happy to have Father Ted and me, his wonderful dog.

And that is my favorite thing.

Ginger,

A dog who found her way into the hearts of many
Who is Ginger?
Loving and fun,
Friendly to many.
But loyal and devoted to her owner.
Curious and smart.
Loves to play, chews on socks,
And wags her tail.
With ears that listen
To footsteps approaching,
Or squirrels scurrying.
Good at chasing rabbits,
Groundhogs, and geese,
Never harming, just enjoying
Every minute of her work.
Looks forward to walks
In parks or down halls
Greeting all who pass by.
Likes her warm bed curling up
In blankets piled high for a little nap.
Loved by all as she is gentle and kind.
—Joy Peeler

Epilogue

Father Ted and Ginger continue to be part of their lovely church. Ginger can be seen on Sundays and other days doing her job of making all the people in the church and community happy.

Questions for Discussion

- How did Ginger change Father Ted's life?

- What do you do when you are sad or when you are happy?

- What do you think your pet does while you are away at school?

- Tell me how your pet makes you feel?

- Tell me three things you like about Ginger.

- Tell me two things you like about Father Ted.

- Write a story or poem about your pet or Ginger.

Acknowledgments

I would like to thank Gretchen and the Russo family for the photos in this book. Thank you to Liz for her technical assistance and a big appreciation to another—you know who you are.